J 808.2 KEN
Kenny, Karen
Cool Scripts & Acting

W9-CQZ-978

DATE DUE

GAYLORD | | PRINTED IN U.S.A.

COOL
Scripts & Acting

How to Stage Your Very Own Show

Karen Latchana Kenney

Consulting Editor, Diane Craig, M.A./Reading Specialist

ABDO
Publishing Company

Visit us at www.abdopublishing.com

Published by ABDO Publishing Company,
8000 West 78th Street, Edina, Minnesota 55439.
Copyright © 2010 by Abdo Consulting Group, Inc.
International copyrights reserved in all countries. No part
of this book may be reproduced in any form without written
permission from the publisher. The Checkerboard Library™
is a trademark and logo of ABDO Publishing Company.

Printed in the United States.
Design and Production: Colleen Dolphin, Mighty Media, Inc.
Photo Credits: Colleen Dolphin, Shutterstock
Series Editor: Katherine Hengel, Pam Price
Activity Production: Britney Haeg

Library of Congress Cataloging-in-Publication Data

Kenney, Karen Latchana.
  Cool scripts & acting : how to stage your very own show / Karen
Latchana Kenney.
    p. cm. -- (Cool performances)
  Includes index.
  ISBN 978-1-60453-717-8
  1. Playwriting--Juvenile literature. 2. Acting--Juvenile literature.
I. Title. II. Title: Cool scripts and acting.

PN1661.K46 2010
808.2--dc22
                                        2009000406

Note to Adult Helpers

When it comes to putting on a show,
scripts and acting are important!
Before beginning, find a good place
for kids to work. If they are going to
play acting games, they will need an
open area. Also, make sure they have
plenty of writing materials for their
scripts. Remind kids to clean up after
themselves, and help them scrounge
around for materials for acting games.
Finally, don't forget to encourage kids
to use their imaginations as they work!

Get the Picture!

There are many activities and how-to photos
in this title. Each how-to photo has a color
border around it, so match the border color
to the appropriate activity step!

1 activity step

Contents

CREATING COOL PERFORMANCES

What's it all about?

Imagine putting on your very own show! Performing in front of an **audience** sounds fun, right? It is! You can pretend to be anything you want to be. Create an **illusion** through your costume, makeup, and stage. Tell a story by acting out a script. Put everything together, and you have a cool show!

You can create many kinds of shows. You can tell a funny story or a serious story. Put on a musical or a fairy tale. Creep out your audience with a monster or a ghost story. You can even be an alien on a strange planet!

Cool Performances Series

Cool Costumes	Cool Scripts & Acting
Cool Makeup	Cool Sets & Props
Cool Productions	Cool Special Effects

Permission

Before beginning, find out if you have permission to put on a show. Ask an adult if you can invite some friends over to talk about your script and play acting games. Make sure you ask for permission to use materials as props.

Safety

Acting games can get a little wild! Make sure you have an open area where you can play. Be careful with the prop pieces you are using. When you are playing acting games, encourage your friends. Don't hurt anyone's feelings. Remember that some people are more shy than others!

Clean Up

- Put away all materials.
- Clean up your work space.
- Throw away paper scraps.
- Wipe down work surfaces.

Show Styles

There are many show styles. Shows can be one style or a combination of styles. Here are just a few.

Drama

Emotions are important in a drama. A dramatic show might be sad or it could make audiences laugh!

Fairy Tale

Fairy tales teach lessons. They have make-believe characters such as fairies, unicorns, and goblins.

Fantasy

Imaginary creatures make this kind of show fantastic! Mad scientists create monsters in laboratories, and aliens fly through space!

Musical

Singing is just as important as acting in a musical. Songs tell parts of the story.

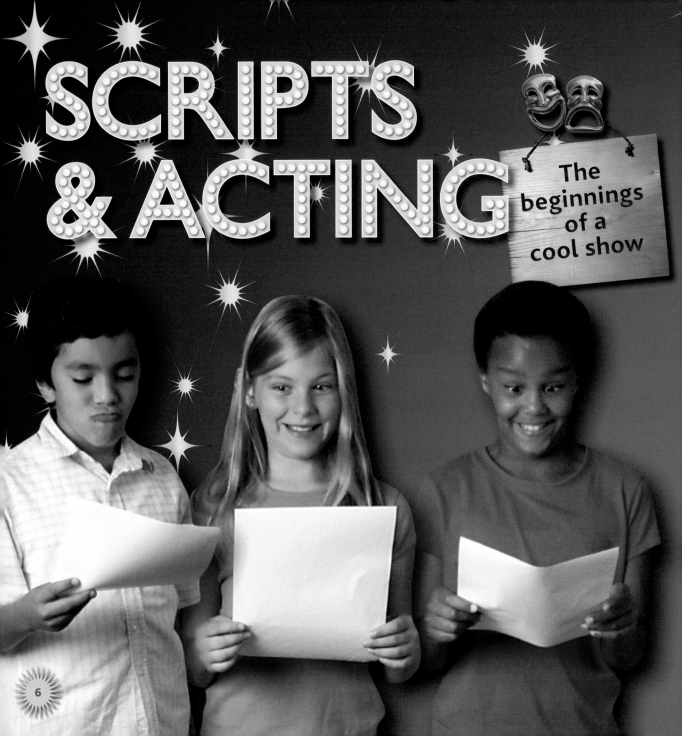

SCRIPTS & ACTING

The beginnings of a cool show

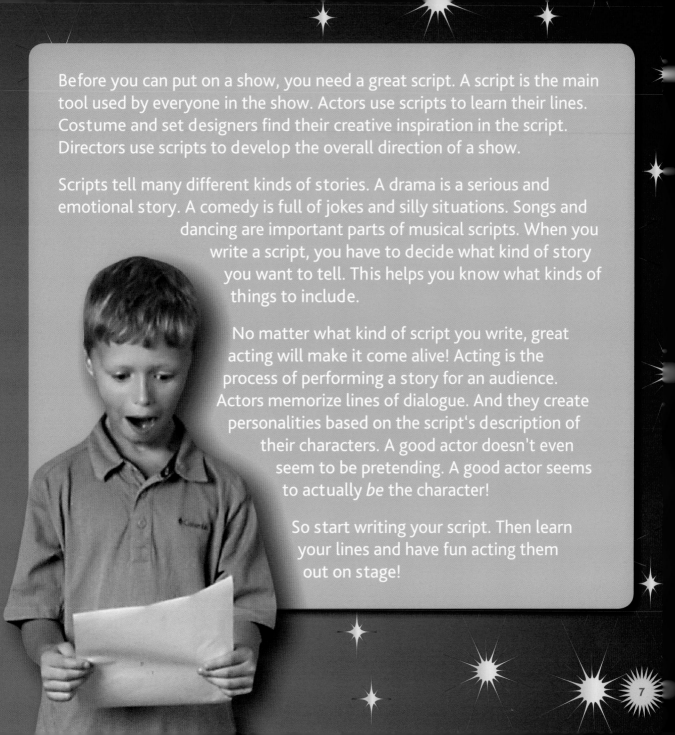

Before you can put on a show, you need a great script. A script is the main tool used by everyone in the show. Actors use scripts to learn their lines. Costume and set designers find their creative inspiration in the script. Directors use scripts to develop the overall direction of a show.

Scripts tell many different kinds of stories. A drama is a serious and emotional story. A comedy is full of jokes and silly situations. Songs and dancing are important parts of musical scripts. When you write a script, you have to decide what kind of story you want to tell. This helps you know what kinds of things to include.

No matter what kind of script you write, great acting will make it come alive! Acting is the process of performing a story for an audience. Actors memorize lines of dialogue. And they create personalities based on the script's description of their characters. A good actor doesn't even seem to be pretending. A good actor seems to actually *be* the character!

So start writing your script. Then learn your lines and have fun acting them out on stage!

PARTS OF A SCRIPT

The roadmap of your show

Scripts contain many important pieces of information. Here are some descriptions of the main parts of a script!

Title The title should say a lot about your show. It should be connected to the story. It could have a main character's name in it. Or it could tell something about the plot. A great title makes your audience curious to see your show!

Playwright The playwright is the person who wrote the play.

Plot To quickly understand what happens in the story, read the plot. It briefly describes important events and characters in the show.

Setting The setting describes where and when a show takes place. It might describe the town, season, or time of day in which the story occurs.

Background Background information tells us what was happening in the characters' lives before the events that occur in the script. Playwrights add background information to help the director and actors understand the story better.

Characters Actors play the characters in a show. The script names and briefly describes each character. Knowing the age, look, personality, and **quirks** of the character helps the actor perform the role.

Acts Shows are sometimes separated into sections called acts. Use **Roman numerals** to label the acts. The first act would be "Act I." The second act would be "Act II."

Scenes An act can be divided into different parts. These parts are called scenes. Use **Arabic numerals** to label scenes. For example, the first scene would be "Scene 1." The second scene would be "Scene 2."

Stage Directions Stage directions tell the actors where and how to move on stage. Stage directions appear in **parentheses** before and after an actor's lines.

Dialogue Dialogue is what characters say in the show. When actors read their lines, they are performing the dialogue.

A LOOK AT A SCRIPT

How a script should look

Title → **Sleeping Judy**

by Katie and Jack ← Playwrights

Plot

Plot

A kind queen gave birth to a beautiful princess. Everyone loved her, except for one very jealous fairy. She placed a curse on the princess! According to the curse, the princess would fall into a deep sleep if she ever pricked her finger on a spindle. Eventually, the princess did prick her finger, but a good fairy who loved the princess very much saved her!

Setting

Setting

Long ago in a great castle on a hill. A town is at the bottom of the hill.

Background

Background

For many years, the kind king and queen were unable to have children. When Judy was finally born, they were very happy. The good fairy was very happy too. She knew the king when he was a baby!

Characters

Characters

JUDY: A beautiful princess. The only child of the king and queen. She is curious and kind. She always likes to explore.

THE KING: Judy's father. He loves his daughter very much. He has a big beard and a loud laugh.

THE QUEEN: Judy's mother. A sweet woman who always wanted a daughter. She has long hair and wears beautiful gowns.

GOOD FAIRY: A fairy that is wise and good. She has pretty wings and sparkles in the light.

BAD FAIRY: A fairy that is evil and jealous. She has shriveled wings and looks green and moldy.

OLD WOMAN: A servant in the castle who has gray hair worn in a tight bun.

ACT I, Scene 1 ←

NARRATOR

One day when her parents were gone, Judy decided to explore the castle.
There were places deep in the castle that she had never seen.
She soon wandered into a tower and found a small door. She peeked
inside and saw an old woman doing something very peculiar.

Stage Directions →

JUDY

(Peeking around the door and looking surprised)
Oh, hello! What is that strange thing you are doing?

OLD WOMAN

Why, I'm spinning thread. Haven't you ever seen a spindle before?

THE KING

(Walking in the door)
Judy! Where has my princess disappeared to? Judy!

Dialogue

BAD FAIRY

(Popping out from behind the door)
Your sweet princess will soon be sleeping for a very long time.
(With an evil laugh, the fairy runs out of the castle)

THE KING

Oh no! Judy, where are you?

GOOD FAIRY

(Suddenly appearing)
Don't worry kind King. I will save the princess!

PLAYING YOUR PART

The scoop on acting

Acting is one of the most important parts of a production. An actor's lines tell the story. That's why the way that actors move and express themselves is so significant. You need to have the right actors playing the right roles. That's how you put on a great show!

Professional shows have a casting director. The casting director helps the director pick actors to be in the show. Together they decide who should play each role. An actor auditions for a role by reading a script. The auditions for your show can be simple. Get your friends together and read the character descriptions. Ask your friends which characters they want to play. If two people want to play a fairy, just have two fairies instead of one. If your friends really like their characters, they will do a better job at playing them!

Once you know which part you're playing, it's time to study the script. Study your lines carefully and try to memorize them. You need to know your lines, and you need to know when to say them. You might have to read the script many times.

Get comfortable with your lines, and then start practicing with the other actors. This is called rehearsing. You will need to rehearse your play at least once before your big performance. Before the show, you will need to "get into character." This means developing the way you look, talk, and move. If your character is from the South, practice talking in a Southern accent. If you are playing an old person, try using a cane to walk. Consider using a facial **twitch** to play someone who is nervous.

Study real people to get your inspiration. Try copying the way they talk or move while you are in front of a mirror. All of these things will make your character more believable.

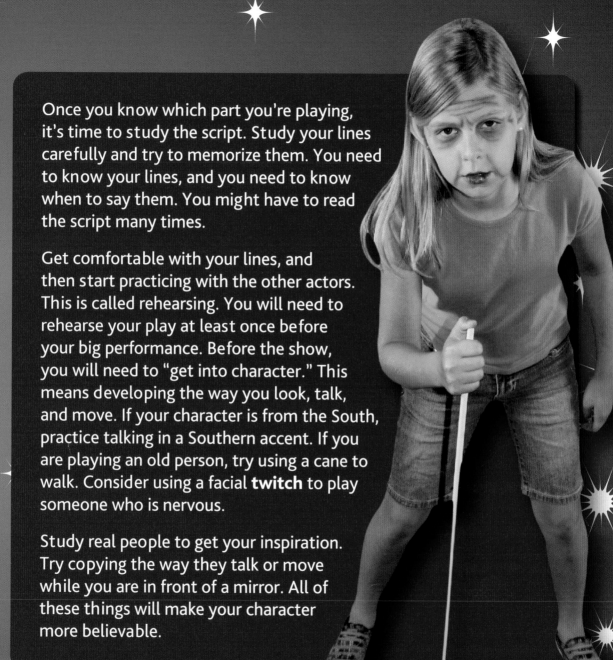

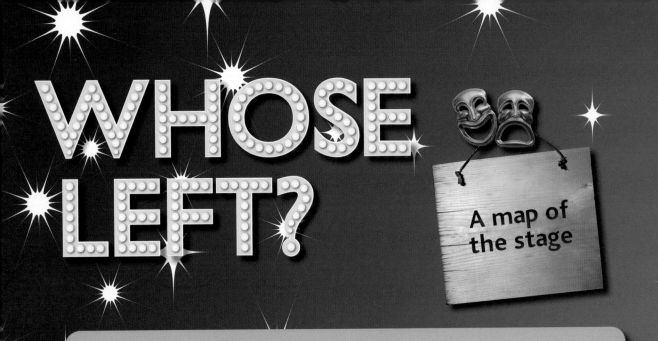

WHOSE LEFT?

A map of the stage

Each area on a stage has a name. These names are called stage directions. Directors use stage directions to tell actors where to stand or move. Years ago, stages were slanted. The back part was higher than the front. That is why the back of the stage is called upstage and the front is called downstage.

Today most stages are flat, but these names are still used. The areas behind the curtains on each side of the stage are called the wings. This is where the actors wait for their cue to go on stage. Stage directions are always from the actor's point of view, so the actor never has to wonder if "upstage left" means the actor's left or the audience's left! Try to learn the parts of the stage. It makes rehearsing a lot easier!

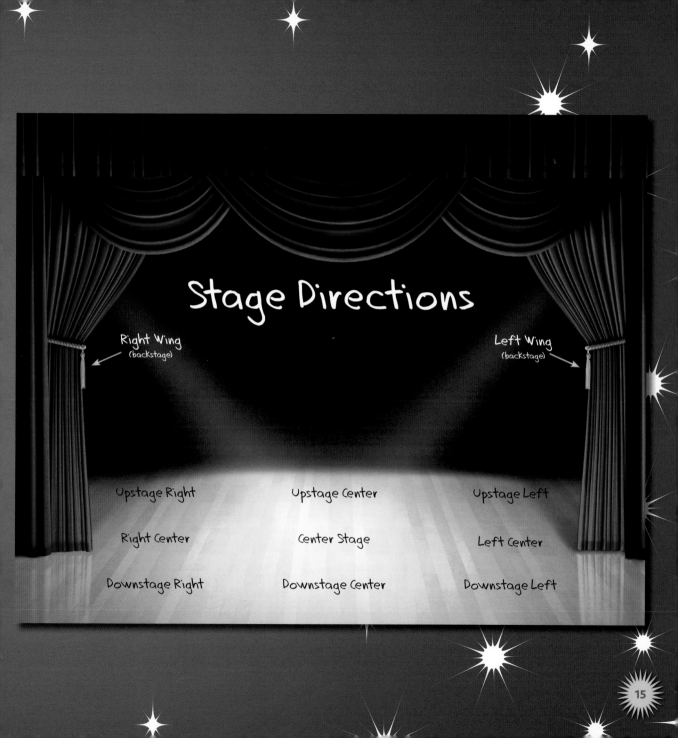

Stage Directions

Right Wing
(backstage)

Left Wing
(backstage)

Upstage Right   Upstage Center   Upstage Left

Right Center   Center Stage   Left Center

Downstage Right   Downstage Center   Downstage Left

Adapt-a-Story

To put on your production, you need a script. Try changing your favorite story into a script!

STAGE KIT

- your favorite short story
- notebook
- pen or pencil

Sleeping Judy

By: Katie and Jack

Reread your favorite short story. As you read, make notes about what is happening on each page. If the story is really long, just pick a section of it to describe.

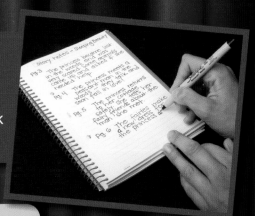

Now it's time to turn your notes into a script. Look at your notes. Decide what the main parts of the story are. On a fresh page in your notebook, write *Plot*. Then describe what happens in the story.

Now write *Setting* in your notebook. Describe where and when your story takes place. Does your story take place in a castle? A haunted house? Does it take place in the future or the past? Add as many details as you can!

Script Notes

See page 11 for an example of how to write **narrator** and character dialogue in your script. Make set pieces and props that match the **setting** of the script. See the book *Cool Sets & Props* for ideas.

Now make a character list. Write *Characters* in your notebook. Then list all the characters in the story. Next to each name, describe what the character is like. Are they nice or mean? Young or old? Describe what makes each character different. See page 10 for an example of a character list.

Script Notes

If you write a great play or novel, you do not want others to copy it! Copyright law prevents other people from copying your work. But sometimes you can legally borrow copyrighted material. This is called "fair use." For example, if you use copyrighted material for an educational or research purpose, it is usually considered fair use. To learn more about copyrights and fair use, visit www.copyrightkids.org.

Now it's time to write lines for your characters. These lines will tell your story! Write the character's name before the lines that you want that character to say. You can add stage directions that tell actors where to go. Stage directions should be put in **parentheses**. You can also use a **narrator** to help tell your story. Here's an example:

NARRATOR
One day when her parents were gone, Judy decided to explore the castle.

JUDY
(Upstage left. Peeking around the door and looking surprised)
Oh, hello! What is that strange thing you are doing?

OLD WOMAN
Why, I'm spinning thread! Haven't you ever seen a spindle before?

When you are finished writing your script, reread it to make sure it makes sense. You now have the first **draft** of your script!

Write-a-Script

Are you ready to write your own story? Grab a notebook and pen and start writing down your ideas. You have to start somewhere!

STAGE KIT

- notebook
- pen or pencil

Characters

Jane: can play Princess Judy. She has curly blond hair and likes to wear dresses. She is kind and curious and loves to explore!

Jack: can play either Prince John or the King. He is very brave but also kind and gentle. He also has a loud voice that sounds like a king!

Katie: can play the Bad Fairy. She likes to play the angry, evil roles because she can make her voice sound really scary! She is also really dramatic!

Emily: can play one of the Good Fairies. She has played a fairy before and is good at it! She is quiet and can flutter around, just like a real fairy.

Billy: can be the narrator. He loves to tell stories and is a good speaker. He is good at memorizing stories, too. He's very funny, too!

Think of an interesting plot. Your plot needs to have a conflict. A conflict is a problem or a question that needs to be solved. Check out "Cool Story Starters" for ideas.

Think of the characters that will be in your show. See how many of your friends can join your show. Then create characters for them. Describe their ages, personalities, looks, and **unique quirks**!

Decide on a **setting** for your script. Imagine what your show will look like on stage. Describe all the details.

Write the lines for each character. Follow the steps in the "Adapt-a-Story" activity on pages 16 –19. You might want to break your show into scenes or acts. Keep writing and soon you'll have your own script. Congratulations!

Cool Story Starters

Use these ideas to start writing your own script!

Lost in Space!

Two aliens are flying to Mars. Suddenly, their space ship breaks down, and they start falling towards Earth!

A Witch's Spell

Two kids stumble upon a strange cottage. They meet a strange woman stirring something in a big pot. The bubbling mixture splashes onto their hands! Soon, there are green warts growing on their hands!

Fairy Flowers

A quiet woman has a secret garden that she rarely lets anyone see. Three friends sneak into the garden through a hole in the fence. They discover a fairy town in the woman's tulip patch!

The Brave Knight

Three boys are training to become knights. Two are show-offs. The third is polite and kind. What happens when a dangerous dragon shows up in the village?

Picture Script

Draw a storyboard to show your script in pictures! A storyboard is a series of pictures that tell a story. It is kind of like a comic book. Drawing a storyboard can help develop the story. It's also helpful when you make the props and set pieces.

1 opening scene

2 fairies in the forest

3 meeting in the forest

4 the spindle

5 castle under sleep spell

6 fighting the dragon

7 Judy awakens

8 final scene

STAGE KIT
- plain piece of paper
- pen or pencil
- markers or colored pencils

Use a black marker to divide a piece of paper into eight rectangles as shown. Number the rectangles one through eight.

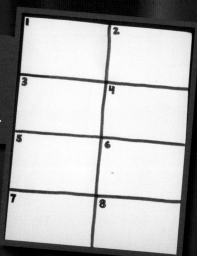

Draw a scene from your show in each rectangle. The first rectangle should show the opening scene. The last should show the final scene.

Think about the kinds of sets and props you will need to make. Also think about stage directions for your characters. If a part of the story doesn't seem to flow, you may need to change your script.

When you are happy with your storyboard, color in your drawings. Show the storyboard to everyone involved in your show. It will help them understand your vision!

ZipZapZop

1. Get a group of friends together. Sit in a circle. Choose someone to be the game starter. The game starter claps and says, "Zip!" and points to another player. That player claps and says, "Zap!" and points to another player. That player claps and says, "Zop!" and points to another player. That player starts over with "Zip!"

2. When someone says the wrong word, he or she is out. The winner is the last one still in the game. Keep the game moving quickly to make it more fun!

Not My Hands

STAGE KIT
- a partner
- an audience
- table
- glass of water
- comb

1 You will need a partner and an audience for this game. Place several props on a table. Try a glass of water and a comb.

2 Stand behind the table, facing the audience. Clasp your hands behind your back. Your partner stands behind you and puts his or her arms through your elbows. It should look like your partner's hands are your hands!

3 Now it's time to improvise! As your partner picks up props from the table, you have to react! The clumsy hands that appear to be yours will surely make your audience laugh!

It's How You Say It

Sometimes it's not what you say. It's how you say it! Try showing different emotions while saying the same phrase.

1 Get a group of three or more people together. Sit in a circle.

2 Divide a piece of paper in half. On the left side, write six different emotions. On the right side, write six different phrases.

3 Use a scissors to cut out each emotion and each phrase. Put all the emotions in one pile. Put all the phrases in another pile.

Surprised	Your dog was dancing by my door
Crabby	You have spaghetti on your face!
Excited	My gerbil loves to eat tacos.
Confused	The princess pulled cupcakes from her hair
Bored	I saw an alien in the alley
Sad	Standing on my head makes me dizzy

Character Characteristics

Observe people to see what is **unique** about them. These things are parts of their character. Use your observations or some items from this list to add to your character.

- facial **twitch**
- speaking accent
- hair twirling
- throat clearing
- nervous laughter
- finger tapping
- eyebrow wrinkling
- confident walking
- squinty eyes

4 Ask each person in the circle to pick out a phrase. Put the emotions in the middle of the circle.

5 To start the game, pick an emotion. Then stand up and say your phrase using that emotion! Experiment with the sound of your voice. Make different faces. Imagine feeling that emotion!

6 See if anyone in your group can guess what emotion you are trying to show. If no one can, then try using another emotion with the same phrase. If someone guesses correctly, it's his or her turn to act!

Stage Whisper

A stage whisper is not really a whisper. It is a way of talking in a hushed voice. The audience can still hear what you are saying though.

1 Open your mouth and start breathing loudly. Use your breath more than your voice as you try to speak.

2 The words will sound **raspy**. The audience will hear what you're saying, but it will not sound the same as regular talking.

3 Use your body to add to the **illusion**. Hunch your shoulders over to look secretive. Put one hand by your mouth to look like you are whispering. This is your stage whisper!

8

Projecting Your Voice

Make your voice soar across the audience! Be heard from far away without yelling.

 1 Usually, we use our throats when we talk. To project your voice, you need to use your chest!

 2 Start by loudly saying, "Ha! Ha! Ha!" You will notice that your chest is moving out when you do this. This is speaking from your chest.

 3 Now, try speaking to someone who is standing far away. Ask the person if he or she can hear you. Notice how far away the person is standing. That is the distance your voice is projecting!

CONCLUSION

You have finished your script, practiced your lines, and created your characters. Now it's time for the fun part! You get to act on stage! This is called performing. Have fun with your role and remember your lines. Isn't it cool to play a character?

But you need more than a script and actors to put on a show. Check out the other books in the Cool Performances series to learn more about putting on a show. Learn how to use makeup and costumes to create different looks. Create sets and props. Add lighting and special effects. Promote your show with flyers and a cool banner. Have fun and let your imagination run wild!

GLOSSARY

Arabic numeral – any of the number symbols 0, 1, 2, 3, 4, 5, 6, 7, 8, and 9.

draft – a quickly created sketch or outline from which a final work is produced.

illusion – something that looks real but is not.

narrator – the voice in a story that provides information.

parentheses – a pair of curved marks used to enclose an expression.

quirk – a peculiar trait.

raspy – harsh and scratchy.

Roman numeral – a number that is represented by Roman letters such as I, V, and X.

twitch – to move or pull suddenly.

unique – the only one of its kind.

Web Sites

To learn more about putting on a show, visit ABDO Publishing Company on the World Wide Web at www.abdopublishing.com. Web sites about theater are featured on our Book Links page. These links are routinely monitored and updated to provide the most current information available.

INDEX